HAUNTED AMERICA

GHOSTS OF ALCATRAZ

AND OTHER HAUNTINGS OF THE WEST

by Suzanne Garbe

CAPSTONE PRESS
a capstone imprint

Edge Books are published by Capstone Press,
1710 Roe Crest Drive, North Mankato, Minnesota 56003
www.capstonepub.com

Library of Congress Cataloging-in-Publication Data
Garbe, Suzanne.
  Ghosts of Alcatraz and other hauntings of the West / by Suzanne Garbe.
    pages cm.—(Edge Books. Haunted America)
  Includes index and bibliographical references.
  Summary: "Describes ghost sightings and hauntings in the western United States"—
Provided by publisher.
  ISBN 978-1-4765-3915-7 (library binding)
  ISBN 978-1-4765-5963-6 (ebook pdf)
1. Haunted places—West (U.S.)—Juvenile literature. 2. Ghosts—West (U.S.)—
Juvenile literature. I. Title.
  BF1472.U6.G355 2014
  133.10978—dc23   2013031837

Editorial Credits
Anthony Wacholtz, editor; Heidi Thompson, designer; Svetlana Zhurkin,
media researcher; Danielle Ceminsky, production specialist

Photo Credits
Alamy: Jeff Greenberg, 17; Corbis: Bettmann, 22 (top), 23, ClassicStock, 10–11, Richard
Cummins, 18–19, Underwood & Underwood, 11 (top); Library of Congress, 7 (back),
14–15, 20–21, 22 (bottom); Newscom: Danita Delimont Photography/Alim Kassim,
24–25, Everett Collection, 7 (inset), KRT/Mark Rightmire, 9 (inset), ZUMA Press/
Earl Cryer, 12–13; Shutterstock: Alexey Kamenskiy, 16, Andresr, cover, 4–5, Dmitry
Natashin (frame), 9, 11, 22, Donald R. Neudecker, 6, echo3005 (gates), back cover, 1,
2, 29, Ivakoleva (texture), throughout, littlleny, 26–27, Map Resources, 28, 29, nikkytok
(smoke), throughout, Robert Kelsey, 8–9

Direct Quotations
Page 10: Jeff Belanger. "The World's Most Haunted Places." Rev. ed. Pompton Plains,
N.J.: New Page Book, 2011, 24.
Page 12: Ibid., 245.
Page 19: Ibid., 55.
Page 25: "Southwest Ghost Hunters Association." http://www.sgha.net/az/jerome/
jeromegrand2.html

Printed in the United States of America in Stevens Point, Wisconsin.
092013   007768WZS14

TABLE OF CONTENTS

Nearly every town has a legend about a haunted place. Maybe it's the creepy house on the corner, where a lone figure watches from a second-story window. Perhaps it's the high school auditorium, where the ghost of a former student wanders the stage. Whether or not we believe in ghosts, these stories have the power to haunt us. The United States is home to some of the world's creepiest haunted places. Take a tour of the western United States and explore its stories of ghosts and hauntings.

ALCATRAZ ISLAND

One of the most famous haunted places in the United States is Alcatraz prison. Even before the famous prison was built, Alcatraz Island in California was said to be haunted. According to legend, the Miwok Indians thought evil **spirits** lived there. Historians think the Miwok sent tribe members there to punish them for breaking laws.

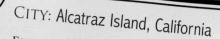

CITY: Alcatraz Island, California

FIRST REPORTED HAUNTING: 1963, maybe earlier

TYPES OF ACTIVITY: screams, crying, music, cold spots

SCARY RANKING: 5

ACCESS: Guided and self-guided tours are available through the National Park Service.

After California became a state in 1850, the federal government built a military fortress on Alcatraz to guard the coast. In the 1860s it became a training site for Union soldiers during the Civil War (1861–1865). Around the same time, a military prison opened on the island.

Alcatraz prison was **renovated** by 1912, becoming the world's biggest reinforced concrete building. Eventually, the cost of bringing fresh water, food, and supplies to the island grew too large. The Army closed the prison and left the island in 1933.

The prison became a federal **penitentiary** in 1934 and was known for its strict security. Many prisoners tried to escape, but there is no evidence that any of them made it out alive. Alcatraz finally closed in 1963.

spirit—the invisible part of a person that contains thoughts and feelings; some people believe the spirit leaves the body after death
renovate—to restore something to good condition
penitentiary—a prison for people found guilty of serious crimes

Visitation windows sat at the end of a hallway lined with cell blocks

Although Alcatraz closed, many people believe ghosts stayed behind. Since the National Park Service took over the island in 1973, numerous visitors have reported signs of **paranormal** activity. Tourists hear the clanging of metal and the cries and screams of inmates. Cell 14-D is often noted to be particularly cold, and several visitors have reported feeling strong emotions inside. The cell held a single prisoner who had no contact with other people for more than three years.

One of Alcatraz's most famous inmates was the gangster Al Capone. He was reported to frequently play the banjo in the prison's shower room. Today visitors report the ghostly sounds of a banjo lingering in the showers.

The paranormal events at Alcatraz have enticed visitors to the island. Some visitors believe the same goes for both ghosts and former prisoners—no one can escape from Alcatraz.

Al Capone

paranormal—having to do with an unexplained event that has no scientific explanation

STANLEY HOTEL

Brothers Francis and F. O. Stanley made a fortune after inventing a steam-powered car, the Stanley Steamer. F. O. took his wealth and moved to Estes Park, Colorado. He built the Stanley Hotel, a resort with stunning views of the Rocky Mountains and nearby valleys. It offered guests many activities, including bowling, golf, and orchestra concerts. Guests included former U.S. President Theodore Roosevelt, musician Bob Dylan, and writer Stephen King. King found the hotel to be unsettling and creepy, which inspired him to write his famous book *The Shining*.

King isn't the only one to have felt uneasy at the Stanley Hotel, which is still open today. Guests have reported having their feet tickled during the night and having their luggage mysteriously unpacked. Lights turn on and off by themselves, and children's voices are heard in empty halls. Some visitors have seen the ghost of F. O. walking in the lobby.

CITY: Estes Park, Colorado

FIRST REPORTED HAUNTING: 1950s

TYPES OF ACTIVITY: ghost sightings, voices, ghostly touches, moving objects

SCARY RANKING: 3

ACCESS: Several tour options are available, including history tours and ghost hunt tours; the hotel also takes overnight guests.

Most people who say they've encountered the ghosts believe they're friendly. Some people think the Stanleys and their original staff want to make sure guests have a pleasant stay.

QUEEN MARY SHIP

CITY: Long Beach, California

FIRST REPORTED HAUNTING: 1967

TYPES OF ACTIVITY: ghost sightings, voices, smells, moving objects

SCARY RANKING: 5

ACCESS: Many tour options are available.

After the *Queen Mary* ship was built in the 1930s, it carried movie stars and British royalty between Europe and North America. During World War II (1939–1945), it was briefly painted gray and used to transport soldiers. It then returned to its job of transporting passengers. The *Queen Mary* was bigger than the famous passenger ship *Titanic*, and it was called the most glamorous ship ever built. It stopped running in 1967 after its owners lost too much business to airplane travel.

"The Queen Mary is the most haunted place that I have ever investigated, and I've literally been around the globe with hauntings ... There are at least 600 active resident ghosts on the Queen Mary."
– Peter James, famous psychic

Today the ship is docked in Long Beach, California. It is used as a hotel and party venue. However, its long history seems to have left a few ghosts behind. At one point during the war, the *Queen Mary* crashed into another ship and split it in two. Today visitors report hearing a loud collision and the cries of drowning sailors.

There are also reports of ghosts from the ship's passenger days. Visitors have heard the voice of a young girl who drowned in one of the ship's pools. Staff members have seen waves in the pool and wet footprints near it at night after the pool is locked. Staff members have also seen ghosts of people dressed in old clothing. Workers have even reported **poltergeist** activity, such as plates flying across the room, pictures moving, and doors opening and closing.

Cabin class passengers would gather at one of the lounges for a marvelous view over the bow of the *Queen Mary*.

poltergeist—a ghost that causes physical events, like objects moving

WHALEY HOUSE

Thomas Whaley built the Whaley House in San Diego in 1857. It was one of the finest houses in Southern California. However, the Whaley House was the site of tragedy and death. One of Thomas' sons died at 17 months, and one of his daughters killed herself. Legal problems led to Thomas losing all his money. He became bitter and mean, dying in 1890 at age 67.

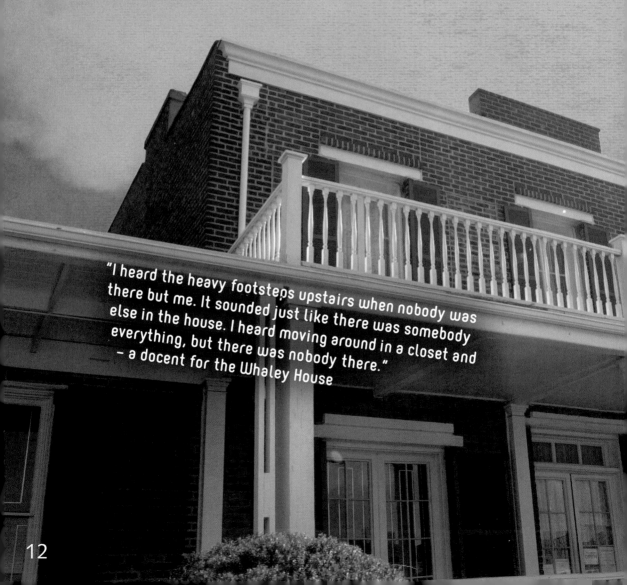

"I heard the heavy footsteps upstairs when nobody was there but me. It sounded just like there was somebody else in the house. I heard moving around in a closet and everything, but there was nobody there."
– a docent for the Whaley House

CITY: San Diego, California

FIRST REPORTED HAUNTING: between 1856 and 1890

TYPES OF ACTIVITY: ghost sightings, smells, odd voices and music, cold spots, mysterious footsteps, ghostly touches

SCARY RANKING: 2

ACCESS: Self-guided and group tours are available.

Today the Whaley House is a museum where visitors can learn about the area's history and the building's ghostly encounters. Many people believe the house is haunted by its tragic past. According to the Whaley House's **docent**, even Thomas Whaley heard mysterious heavy footsteps in the house. Whaley believed that Yankee Jim, an accused thief who had been hanged on the property, was haunting him. Many people think Thomas Whaley and his family haunt the house too. Some have claimed to see the ghost of the Whaleys' infant son.

Visitors have reported various types of strange activity. They claimed to experience cold spots, unexplained lights, and noises with no source. Other visitors have reported hearing phantom piano music and the feeling of people brushing up against them when no one is nearby. One docent saw a room filled with fog that couldn't be explained. Some visitors reported seeing the ghost of a man hanging in a doorway.

WHALEY HOUSE

HISTORICAL LANDMARK NO. 65

docent—a guide at a museum, art gallery, or zoo

THORNEWOOD CASTLE

CITY: Lakewood, Washington

FIRST REPORTED HAUNTING: 2000

TYPES OF ACTIVITY: ghost sightings, moving objects

SCARY RANKING: 1

ACCESS: The castle is a bed-and-breakfast and wedding venue; tours are sometimes offered.

In 1907 wealthy businessman Chester "Ches" Thorne set out to build his dream home. He had an English castle taken apart and shipped piece by piece to Lakewood, Washington. He used a combination of the old pieces and new materials to put the house back together. U.S. presidents Theodore Roosevelt and William Howard Taft visited the house when it was finished.

Ches died in 1927, but some people think his spirit is still in Thornewood Castle. One of the owners believes his ghost is responsible for many strange experiences. She's seen glass break and lightbulbs come unscrewed without reason. Several people have seen a man—thought to be Ches' ghost—in a riding suit and spurs.

Other spirits have been reported wandering Thornewood Castle. Women getting married at the castle have looked in a mirror and seen the image of a woman wearing clothing from the early 1900s. A ghostly woman has been seen looking out a window from the same room.

THE ALASKAN HOTEL

A gold rush brought settlers to Alaska in the late 1800s and early 1900s. In 1913 two brothers built the Alaskan Hotel in Juneau. Miners stayed there between trips into the wild to look for gold. When they found gold, they came back to the hotel to spend it.

Today the Alaskan Hotel & Bar is still open, and it's the longest-operating hotel in the state. Staff and visitors tell many stories of ghostly encounters. Local stories say that a woman, murdered by her jealous husband, haunts the hotel. The hotel's front desk clerk says that Room 219 is always cold. Guests frequently ask to be moved out of the room. Other guests have reported seeing the ghost of a woman who touches them or sits on their beds. Housekeepers say they have put a stack of towels down in one place, only to find them mysteriously appear somewhere else later.

CITY: Juneau, Alaska

FIRST REPORTED HAUNTING: unknown

TYPES OF ACTIVITY: ghost sightings, cold spots, moving objects, ghostly touches

SCARY RANKING: 2

ACCESS: The hotel is open to the public.

BIG NOSE KATE'S SALOON

CITY: Tombstone, Arizona

FIRST REPORTED HAUNTING: unknown

TYPES OF ACTIVITY: ghost sightings, moving objects, mysterious footsteps, ghostly touches

SCARY RANKING: 4

ACCESS: The restaurant and bar are open to the public.

The gunfight at the O.K. Corral is one of the most famous in U.S. history. The event took place in 1881 in Tombstone, Arizona Territory, between lawmen and bandits. Before the gunfight, the bandits stayed at the Grand Hotel in Tombstone. The hotel burned down in 1882 and was replaced by Big Nose Kate's Saloon, which is still open today.

Visitors to Big Nose Kate's have spotted the **apparitions** of bandits. They've been seen perched on bar stools and spilling drinks in the basement. Guests have had their hair pulled and seen chairs and bar stools move without being touched. Lights turn on and off, and boot steps echo across the dance floor. Bartenders count the number of glasses that fly across the room without being touched. The ghost of an old miner nicknamed "Swamper" has also been seen throughout the building. Legends say he buried silver in the building and has stayed to protect it.

"I've had them [ghosts] yank my hair back, touch me, walk by me when there's no one there. Chairs beside me move like someone just walked up and pulled out a chair to sit down."
— Tricia Rawson, Tombstone tour guide

apparition—the visible appearance of a ghost

19

WINCHESTER MYSTERY HOUSE

CITY: San Jose, California

FIRST REPORTED HAUNTING: 1884

TYPES OF ACTIVITY: ghost sightings, ghostly voices and music, balls of light, strange smells

SCARY RANKING: 4

ACCESS: The house is open daily for tours.

The Winchester Mystery House is an impressive structure, but it has an eerie past. The house's creator, Sarah Pardee, married William Wirt Winchester in 1862 in New Haven, Connecticut. William's father owned the gun company that made the popular Henry Repeater. It was a gun sometimes used by the Union army during the American Civil War. The Henry Repeater made the Winchesters rich, but nothing could protect them from tragedy. In 1866 Sarah gave birth to a daughter who lived only a few days. Fifteen years later, William died of tuberculosis.

Sarah never recovered from the losses of her daughter and husband. A **medium** told Sarah she was cursed by the ghosts of soldiers, American Indians, and others killed by her husband's rifles. The medium said she should head west and build a home for all the ghosts. Sarah followed the advice.

In 1884 Sarah moved from Connecticut to California and bought an eight-room home in San Jose. She then decided to expand the house. She thought that it would confuse the ghosts, making it hard for them to reach her.

Sarah Winchester

Sarah's bedroom

For the next 38 years, the house was under constant construction. Sarah built staircases that led to nowhere and hallways that doubled back on themselves. She added rooms with no plan or purpose. She built dozens of chimneys so the ghosts could come and go. Sarah lived in the house as a **recluse** until her death in 1922. At that point, the house had about 160 rooms.

A visitor to the Winchester Mystery House explores a set of stairs that end at the ceiling.

Sarah Winchester wasn't the only person to believe the house is filled with ghosts. Since Sarah's death, visitors to the house have reported many eerie encounters. They have seen mysterious balls of light and the ghosts of a gray-haired woman and a workman wearing coveralls. Visitors have also heard phantom voices, ghostly music, and slamming doors. They've even smelled freshly cooked soup in kitchens that haven't been used for decades.

medium—a person who claims to communicate with the spirits of dead people
recluse—a person who lives alone and avoids other people

JEROME GRAND HOTEL

The Jerome Grand Hotel had a long history before it became a hotel in 1994. It was originally built in 1926 as a hospital that served Jerome, Arizona. When mining ended in the city in 1950, the hospital closed. The building sat empty for decades.

As soon as the hospital was turned into a hotel in 1994, ghost reports began flooding in. Visitors have seen the ghost of a nurse wandering around the hotel. They've also seen the ghost of a woman who roams the halls and asks for help finding her lost baby. Guests report hearing wheezing, coughs, and voices. Some visitors have felt a child's hand touch them. Others have seen the apparition of a small boy and reported the smell of a hospital. Guests have also been pinched and felt mysterious weights on their beds at night. Many people believe the hotel will forever be haunted by those who died there when it was a hospital.

CITY: Jerome, Arizona

FIRST REPORTED HAUNTING: 1994

TYPES OF ACTIVITY: ghost sightings, voices, smells, ghostly touches

SCARY RANKING: 5

ACCESS: Ghost tours are available.

"The most common occurrence is the sound of labored breathing and coughing coming from empty rooms. Worse, these sounds often **emanate** from a dark corner of a guest's room."
– Southwest Ghost Hunters Association, describing a 2005 study at the hotel

emanate—to spread out from a source

ROOSEVELT HOTEL

CITY: Hollywood, California

FIRST REPORTED HAUNTING: 1985

TYPES OF ACTIVITY: ghost sightings, cold spots, lights turning on and off

SCARY RANKING: 4

ACCESS: The hotel is open to the public.

The Roosevelt Hotel opened in 1927 as a hotel for glamorous Hollywood film stars. The first Academy Awards ceremony was held at the Roosevelt in 1929. Marilyn Monroe lived there for two years at the start of her modeling career. Other movie stars from the 1930s and 1940s, such as Clark Gable and Carole Lombard, also stayed at the Roosevelt.

Today the rich and famous continue to stay at the Roosevelt. However, the hotel is known for more than its star guests. Visitors began to report paranormal events in 1985 after the hotel was renovated. Staff and visitors have claimed to see Marilyn Monroe's face in a mirror. Some guests have seen the ghost of Hollywood star Montgomery Clift pacing in the hallway. The ghost of Carole Lombard, who died at age 33 in a plane crash in 1942, has also been spotted. One guest even brought a Ouija board to the hotel to try to contact Montgomery Clift. She left at 4:00 a.m. in a panic after her room's lights and coffee pot turned themselves on and off.

HAUNTED PLACES IN THIS BOOK

Alaska

The Alaskan Hotel

OTHER HAUNTED LOCATIONS OF THE WEST

- San Francisco-Oakland Bay Bridge in San Francisco Bay, California
- Mission La Purisima in Lompoc, California
- Hotel del Coronado in Coronado, California
- McMenamin's Grand Lodge in Forest Grove, Oregon
- The Bush House in Index, Washington
- Rutherglen Mansion Bed and Breakfast in Longview, Washington
- USS *Arizona* in Pearl Harbor, Hawaii
- The Hearthstone Inn in Colorado Springs, Colorado
- Old Idaho Penitentiary in Boise, Idaho
- Little Bighorn Battlefield National Monument in Crow Agency, Montana
- Ivy House Inn Bed and Breakfast in Casper, Wyoming

Thornewood Castle

Washington

Montana

Oregon

Idaho

Wyoming

California

Nevada

Alcatraz Island
Winchester Mystery House

Stanley Hotel

Utah

Colorado

Roosevelt Hotel
Queen Mary Ship

Arizona

New Mexico

Whaley House

Jerome Grand Hotel

Big Nose Kate's Saloon

29

GLOSSARY

apparition (ap-uh-RISH-uhn)—the visible appearance of a ghost

docent (DOE-sent)—a guide at a museum, art gallery, or zoo

emanate (EM-uh-nate)—to spread out from a source

medium (MEE-dee-um)—a person who claims to communicate with the spirits of dead people

paranormal (pair-uh-NOHR-muhl)—having to do with an unexplained event that has no scientific explanation

penitentiary (pen-uh-TEN-chur-ee)—a prison for people found guilty of serious crimes

poltergeist (POLL-ter-guyst)—a ghost that causes physical events, such as objects moving

recluse (RECK-loose)—a person who lives alone and avoids other people

renovate (REH-no-vate)—to restore something to good condition

venue (VEN-yoo)—the place where an event happens

spirit (SPIHR-it)—the invisible part of a person that contains thoughts and feelings; some people believe the spirit leaves the body after death

READ MORE

Belanger, Jeff. *The World's Most Haunted Places.* Haunted: Ghosts and the Paranormal. New York: Rosen Publishing, 2009.

Chandler, Matt. *The World's Most Haunted Places.* The Ghost Files. Mankato, Minn.: Edge Books. 2012.

Everett, J.H., and Marilyn Scott-Waters. *Haunted Histories: Creepy Castles, Dark Dungeons, and Powerful Palaces.* New York: Henry Holt and Company, 2012.

INTERNET SITES

FactHound offers a safe, fun way to find Internet sites related to this book. All of the sites on FactHound have been researched by our staff.

Here's all you do:

Visit www.facthound.com

Type in this code: 9781476539157

Check out projects, games and lots more at
www.capstonekids.com

INDEX